PIONEERS IN MEDICINE

By Susan Brocker and Kathy Furgang

TABLE OF CONTENTS

INTRODUCTION

A pioneer blazes a trail that others can follow. Medical pioneers invent, develop, or discover something that leads to a better world for all.

Clara Barton (1821–1912) battlefield nurse and founder of the American Red Cross

**Alexander Fleming
(1881–1955)** bacteriologist
and discoverer of penicillin,
the world's first antibiotic

Charles Drew (1904–1950)
surgeon and researcher
who established the
world's first blood bank

C lara Barton, Alexander Fleming, and Charles Drew were three great medical pioneers. Their work has saved millions of lives. Clara Barton was an American nurse, Alexander Fleming was a Scottish **bacteriologist** (bak-teer-ee-AH-luh-jist), and Charles Drew was an African American surgeon. Although they worked in different areas of medicine, they shared a goal: making the world a safer place.

All three people were hardworking, determined, and courageous. Clara Barton helped soldiers on the front lines of battle at a time when women were expected to stay at home. Alexander Fleming worked tirelessly on important experiments that other scientists ridiculed. Charles Drew struggled against racial discrimination to carry out brilliant research. These pioneers left us with three great life-saving gifts: the American Red Cross, **penicillin** (peh-nih-SIH-lin), and **blood banks**.

1

+ + + + + + + + + + + + +

CLARA BARTON

Founder of the American Red Cross 1821–1912

Clara Barton in 1865

A wounded soldier lay where he had fallen, too weak to cry out for help. He could hear the thunder of cannons nearby. He looked up to see a woman. She gave him water and began to treat his wounds. The year was 1862, and the Civil War was raging between the northern and southern states of America. The woman was Clara Barton.

Clara Barton was born in North Oxford, Massachusetts, on Christmas day, 1821. She was the youngest of five children. She loved riding horses bareback and wrestling with her brothers. Although she enjoyed these bold activities, she was very shy.

✛ ✛ ✛ ✛ ✛ ✛ ✛ ✛ ✛ ✛ ✛ ✛ ✛ ✛ ✛ ✛ ✛ ✛

When she was 11, her brother was badly injured in a fall. She volunteered to take care of him. She nursed him day and night for two years. She found that she was good at caring for others and liked the feeling of being needed.

After graduating from school, Barton became a teacher. She was just 17. She often taught for free in poorer areas and set up one of the first free public schools in New Jersey. In spite of all her hard work, a male principal was appointed above her.

✔ Point

Think About It

How do you think Clara Barton felt when a man was appointed above her after all her hard work?

Barton soon moved to Washington, D.C., in search of a new challenge. There she became one of the first women to work for the federal government.

The United States Patent Office looked like this in 1854, when Clara Barton began working there as a clerk.

+ + + + + + + + + + + + + + + + + + +

Angel of the Battlefield

Barton was living in Washington, D.C. when the Civil War broke out. After the first major battle was fought near there, wounded soldiers poured into the city. People set up hospitals in homes, offices, and warehouses. Barton rushed to help. She was shocked at the lack of medical supplies and decided that she had to do something.

She advertised in newspapers for food, clothing, and medical supplies. She organized friends and volunteers to help load the supplies on mule teams. She drove the goods to the army camps and battlefields.

Neither the North nor the South was prepared for the enormous number of wounded soldiers in the war.

+ + + + + + + + + + + + + + + + +

At first, army officials rejected Barton's help. They tried to turn her away. They felt that the front line was no place for a woman and that she would only get in the way. She persisted, however, and was finally allowed to deliver the supplies.

Barton was horrified by the conditions she saw at the front. Wounded soldiers were treated in **field hospitals** that were filthy and overcrowded. On the battlefields, injured soldiers lay for hours and even days without basic medical care, water, or food. There were not enough stretcher teams, medical workers, or supplies.

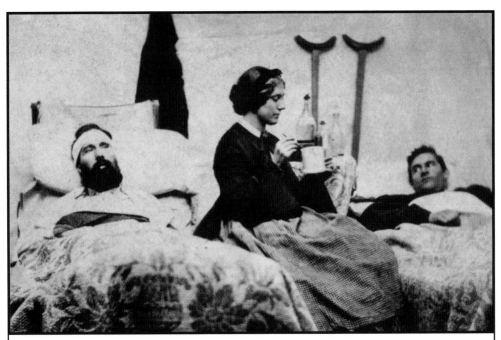

During the Civil War (1861–1865), many women from both sides helped care for wounded soldiers at hospitals. Most of them were not trained nurses, but they assisted in any way they could.

+ + + + + + + + + + + + + + + + + +

IT'S A FACT

The Battle of Antietam was the bloodiest single day of the Civil War. On September 17, 1862, Southern and Northern troops came face-to-face at the village of Sharpsburg, Maryland. By evening, about 4,700 soldiers lay dead. Another 19,000 were injured. From dawn to dusk, Clara Barton worked alongside surgeons, desperately trying to treat thousands of wounded men.

Barton went to work. She brought the soldiers water and food, bathed their wounds, changed their bandages, scrubbed and cleaned the hospitals, and helped the doctors. She also comforted the sick, wounded, and dying men. She read to them, wrote their letters, or just sat and held their hands. She worked without food or rest for days and never seemed to tire.

Sometimes she got so close to the battlefield that she put her own life in danger. She helped surgeons while shells burst overhead and bullets whizzed past. The soldiers nicknamed her their "Angel of the Battlefield."

Today, a memorial at the Antietam National Battlefield marks Clara Barton's courage.

✛ ✛ ✛ ✛ ✛ ✛ ✛ ✛ ✛ ✛ ✛ ✛ ✛ ✛ ✛ ✛

After the war, Barton set up a bureau to search for missing soldiers. She published names of missing men in newspapers and sent them to post offices all over the country. In this way, she helped unite many soldiers with their families.

A former prisoner of war gave Barton a list of soldiers who had died in a prison camp in Andersonville, Georgia. Almost 13,000 had died there from disease and starvation. Barton went to Andersonville and marked the graves of the soldiers. She published their names in newspapers so that people would know where their loved ones were buried.

In August 1866, Clara Barton raised the flag over new headboards that marked the graves of nearly 13,000 soldiers who had died at an Andersonville prison camp.

+ + + + + + + + + + + + + + + + + + +

IT'S A FACT

The emblem of the Red Cross is the Swiss flag with the colors reversed. It was chosen to honor Jean Henri Dunant, the Swiss man who founded the International Red Cross in Geneva, Switzerland, in 1864. All Red Cross workers wear the emblem to set them apart from soldiers on the battlefield. By international agreement, they are protected from attack because they are neutral and unarmed.

The American Red Cross

In 1869, Barton traveled to Switzerland for a well-earned rest. While she was there, she learned about the work of a new organization called the International Red Cross. It had been set up to care for all sick and wounded in times of war, regardless of their nationality.

When war broke out between France and Germany in 1870, Barton went to work again, this time alongside volunteers of the Red Cross. In the cities and towns of France, she helped distribute food and clothing to refugees.

During World War I, Red Cross volunteers worked in war-torn towns and cities helping orphaned children.

+ + + + + + + + + + + + + + + + + +

Barton returned home in 1873, to set up an American branch of the Red Cross. She campaigned hard for many years. She talked to government officials and educated the public about the Red Cross. She wrote articles and gave speeches. She argued that an American Red Cross could help people not only in times of war, but also when natural disasters, such as floods and earthquakes, struck.

She won her battle. In 1881, the American Red Cross was formed. Barton was chosen as president, a post she held for the next 23 years.

Clara Barton's home in Glen Echo, Maryland, served as headquarters for the American Red Cross, as well as a warehouse for disaster relief supplies.

1918

1939

Throughout its history, the American Red Cross has recruited volunteers and contributions by using a series of attractive posters.

The American Red Cross first went into action in the summer of 1881 after fierce forest fires swept through Michigan. The Red Cross gave clothing, blankets, food, and medical supplies to people who had lost their homes.

Over the years, Clara Barton led efforts to help people recover from floods, droughts, tornadoes, and earthquakes across the United States. During a famine in Russia in 1892, she organized a shipment of corn and supplies. As a result of her work, the International Red Cross pledged to help victims of natural disasters as well as war.

In 1900, a flood struck the city of Galveston, Texas. It almost destroyed the city, killing 6,000 people and leaving many homeless. Clara Barton led the Red Cross in setting up soup kitchens, orphanages, and shelters. She was 79 years old.

✚ ✚ ✚ ✚ ✚ ✚ ✚ ✚ ✚ ✚ ✚ ✚ ✚ ✚ ✚ ✚ ✚ ✚

Clara Barton resigned from the Red Cross in 1904. Once again, she sought a new challenge. She found it in setting up the National First Aid Association to teach first aid.

Clara Barton worked to help others in need for most of her life. She once said, "You must never think of anything except the need, and how to meet it."

IT'S A FACT

Each year, the Red Cross helps victims of tens of thousands of disasters all over the world. It recruits millions of people to donate blood. It also teaches people how to prevent and prepare for emergencies by giving courses in first aid and lifesaving skills.

The Red Cross also gives medical aid to countries struck by natural disasters and war. It also helps fight famine and disease.

A Red Cross worker tends to wounded soldiers at an International Field Hospital in Goma, Zaire, in 1994.

ALEXANDER FLEMING

Discoverer of Penicillin

1881–1955

Alexander Fleming in 1951

L ess than 60 years ago, even the smallest cut or scratch could be life-threatening. Tiny living things called **bacteria** could enter a person's body through the cut and cause a serious disease. Scientists were desperately searching for ways to fight these bacteria.

One day in 1928, a bacteriologist named Alexander Fleming noticed a furry mold growing in a dish. His discovery would change the future of medicine and save countless lives.

Alexander Fleming was born at Lochfield Farm in Ayrshire, Scotland, on August 6, 1881. He and his seven brothers and sisters had a happy childhood growing up on the family farm. Fleming was fascinated by animals and plants.

When an uncle died and left him some money, Fleming decided to become a doctor like his older brother. He took lessons and scored at the top on the entrance exams. He went to medical school in London and graduated with honors.

After graduating, he joined the **inoculation** (ih-NAH-kyuh-LAY-shun) department at St. Mary's Hospital as a research assistant. He worked on making and testing new **vaccines** (vak-SEENS). A vaccine contains dead or weakened forms of bacteria or viruses. An injection of vaccine helps the body build up resistance to the disease that the bacteria or viruses cause.

IT'S A FACT

Bacteria are tiny living organisms that can be seen under a microscope. They are all around us—in the soil, on our skin, and in the air. They can multiply very quickly by splitting in two.

There are many types of bacteria. Some cause diseases, such as some kinds of pneumonia. However, most bacteria are not harmful. Some are even helpful. Some turn dead plants and animals into rich soil. Others are necessary for the making of cheese, yogurt, bread, and many medicines.

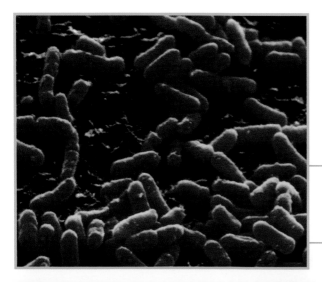

This highly magnified view shows *E. coli*, a common bacteria.

In the laboratory, Fleming studied blood and other body fluids taken from patients. He placed the samples in dishes containing a jelly-like substance that encouraged the bacteria to grow and multiply. He then examined the bacteria under a microscope to find out how they lived and how they might be destroyed.

Fleming, or Little Flem as his workmates called him, was shy, quiet, and hardworking. He was clever with his hands and made glass lab equipment and tiny glass models of cats and dogs. He even grew bacteria in different shapes and colors to create beautiful patterns.

Alexander Fleming sometimes painted pictures using the vibrant colors produced by bacteria he was growing in the laboratory.

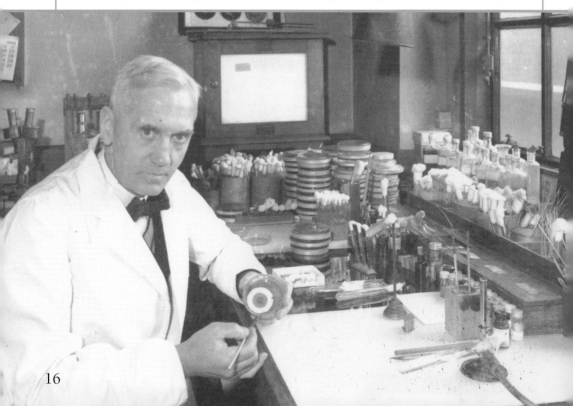

In 1914, World War I broke out. Fleming went to France to treat wounded soldiers. He was shocked by what he saw. Thousands of soldiers died every day from infections caused by bacteria.

Fleming began to wonder if there wasn't something that could fight harmful bacteria without endangering a person's body. Back at St. Mary's, he set to work to find it. In 1921, he discovered **lysozyme** (LY-suh-zime), a natural bacteria-fighter found in body fluids such as tears. Fleming found that lysozyme could dissolve certain types of bacteria. After conducting extensive experiments, however, he concluded that it wasn't strong enough to fight deadly bacteria. He needed to keep searching.

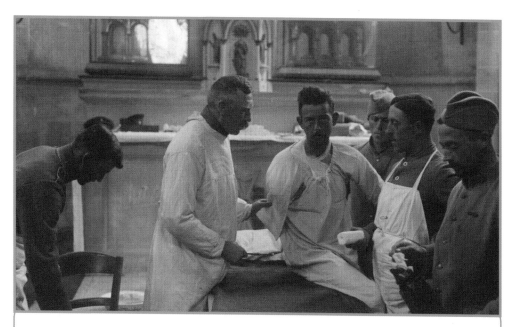

During World War I, doctors used antiseptics to clean wounds and sterilize surgical instruments. Although **antiseptics** killed some bacteria, infection was still a serious problem.

A Lucky Discovery

Fleming often let his bacteria dishes sit for weeks to see if anything interesting would grow. This habit led to his greatest discovery. One morning, he noticed a furry gray-green mold growing on one of the dishes. All around the mold, the bacteria had disappeared. Fleming wondered whether the mold was producing a substance that could kill bacteria.

The mold was called *Penicillium notatum*. It was similar to the mold that grows on rotting fruit. Fleming grew more of the mold so that he could study it.

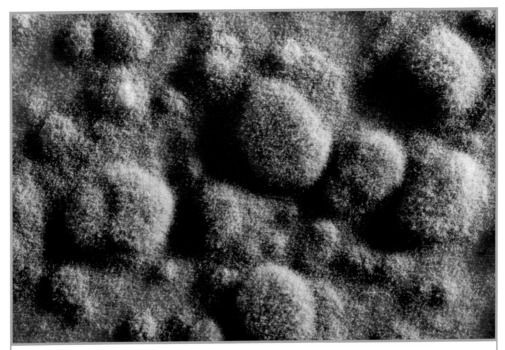

Molds like *Penicillium notatum* grow from tiny **spores.** The spores are floating in the air around us but are much too small to see without a microscope.

Fleming took liquid from the mold and tested it on several types of bacteria. He found that it killed many of the bacteria that cause disease and infections in people. His tests also showed that the liquid did not harm people. He called the liquid penicillin.

Fleming was excited about his discovery, but he couldn't make enough pure penicillin to carry out further tests. In 1929, he wrote a paper and gave lectures about his work, but he couldn't convince other scientists of the importance of his discovery. He returned to his work on vaccines, but he kept a sample of the original mold.

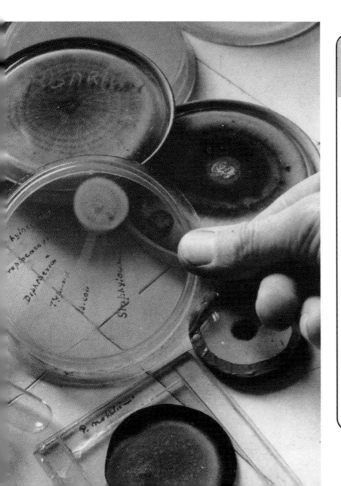

✔ Point

Think About It

The penicillin spores floating in the air landed on Fleming's dish of bacteria quite by accident. Other scientists might have missed seeing the mold, or never allowed it to grow so it could be studied. Was Fleming's discovery simply good luck or good science?

A drugstore manager proudly displays a sign advertising the availability of penicillin in 1945.

Almost 10 years after Fleming's discovery, a team of scientists from Oxford University in England were able to make enough pure penicillin to test it on diseased mice. Every single mouse treated with the drug recovered. Later, they tested it on diseased people with great success.

In 1939, World War II broke out. The new "wonder drug" was used to treat wounded soldiers. With the help of the government, English scientists set up factories to make penicillin. Drug companies in the United States began mass-producing it, too. By the end of the war, penicillin had saved the lives of millions of soldiers.

Since then, penicillin has probably saved more lives than any other drug. Through the use of penicillin and other **antibiotics**, infections that once killed can now be treated.

Alexander Fleming became famous as the discoverer of penicillin. However, he always acknowledged the work of the other scientists. Without them, penicillin might never have been developed as a drug. Fleming once said of his discovery, "Nature makes penicillin; I just found it." In 1945, he was awarded the Nobel Prize for medicine, one of the world's greatest honors.

IT'S A FACT

Drugs that kill bacteria are called antibiotics. After Fleming's discovery, scientists began searching the world for molds, fungi, and other living things that might produce antibiotics. Since that time, thousands of new antibiotics have been developed to treat infections. Unfortunately, bacteria have adapted to many of the antibiotics, making them less effective. New kinds of bacteria that can resist the drugs have evolved.

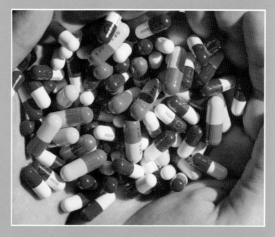

CHARLES DREW

Founder of Blood Banks

1904–1950

Charles Drew

Every day, people donate life-saving blood to hospitals. Until the 1940s, however, donated blood was not useful for very long. If the blood could not be given to a patient within a day or two, it would be wasted. Many lives were lost because not enough blood was available for patients when they needed it.

Thanks to the discoveries of Charles Drew, blood can be preserved long enough to get it to patients in need. The blood banks that Drew established allow hospitals to keep blood on hand for patients who need it.

Charles Richard Drew was born in Washington, D.C., in 1904. He was the oldest of five children. His parents encouraged him to work hard and do well in school.

Drew had a great interest in science and medicine, but he loved athletics, too. In high school he was an award-winning swimmer. He also played basketball, baseball, and football.

Drew attended Amherst College in Massachusetts. In the 1920s, most schools and colleges were **segregated**. Amherst was a school for white students that also accepted some black students, Drew among them.

✔ Point

Read More About It

Using resource materials, read more about the issue of segregation and the fight for equality.

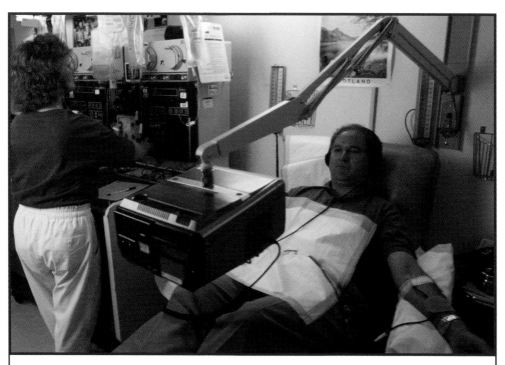

People donate blood to help patients who have had accidents or operations, or who have blood diseases.

Exploring How Blood Works

After graduating from college, Drew taught biology and chemistry at a college in Baltimore, Maryland. He was also the director of athletics at the school. After two years, Drew used his savings to attend medical school in Montreal, Canada.

During class one day, Drew observed a medical procedure that amazed him. He saw a man receive a **blood transfusion**. The patient's blood was replaced by fresh blood that had been donated by another person. Drew knew that getting blood from a donor was difficult. He couldn't help wonder how many lives might be saved if blood could be kept fresh and ready for patients when they needed it.

IT'S A FACT

Blood has four main parts. Red blood cells carry oxygen and wastes throughout the body. White blood cells fight infections and harmful substances that invade the body. Platelets help stop bleeding. Blood cells and platelets move around in a watery liquid called plasma. All parts of blood together are called whole blood.

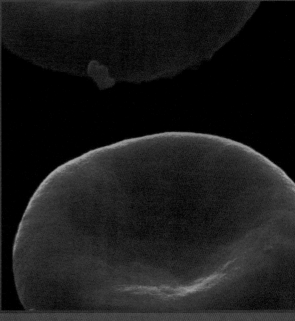

red blood cells seen through a microscope

After medical school, Drew became a teacher at Howard University in Washington, D.C. He also trained at the school's hospital. This gave him experience as a doctor and surgeon. In 1938, he received a fellowship to do research at Columbia University in New York. Now he had his chance to study blood and its parts.

Drew knew that blood would spoil after being taken from a donor. His experiments showed that **plasma,** or the liquid part of blood, lasts longer than whole blood. When plasma was separated from whole blood and each part was refrigerated separately, each part lasted a longer time. The parts could then be recombined and used in a blood transfusion a week later.

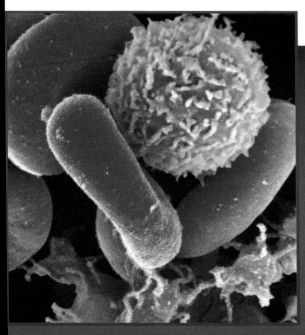

white blood cell seen through a microscope

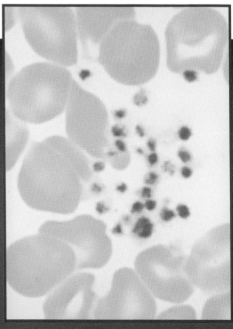

platelet seen through a microscope

IT'S A FACT

How is your blood different from someone else's? Your red blood cells make it different! Scientists have classified all blood into four groups. The groups are named A, B, AB, and O. Only certain blood types can be accepted by certain patients. When someone receives a transfusion, it is very important to know the blood type of the patient and the donor. A patient who is given the wrong type blood could die.

Saving Many Lives

Drew's discovery meant that blood could now be saved until it was needed. People could donate small amounts of their own blood to be stored away for those who would need it at a later time. Many lives could be saved. Drew called this plan a blood bank.

In 1939, World War II was breaking out in Europe. Leaders in Britain heard of Drew's work and asked him to help set up a blood bank for their soldiers in battle. Drew's work with blood banks in Britain gained him recognition around the world.

Citizens donated blood during World War II to be given to soldiers injured in battle.

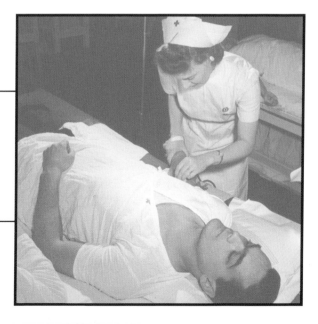

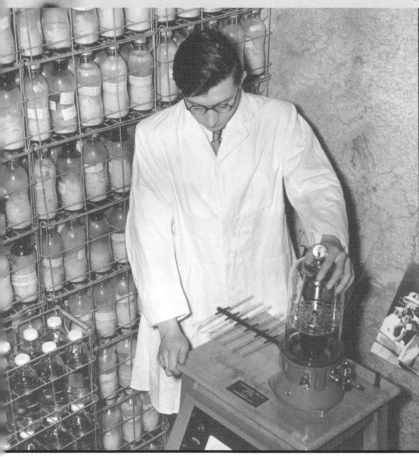

blood bank
around 1948

A few years later, the United States entered World War II. Drew led the American Red Cross in setting up blood banks for American soldiers overseas. However, military officials wanted the Red Cross to keep blood from African Americans separate from blood from people of other races. Drew became angry at this suggestion and later resigned from his position at the Red Cross. His years of research had shown that blood plasma is the same from person to person. It does not matter what race, sex, or age the donor is. The primary concern is that the blood type of the donor is a match with that of the patient.

27

IT'S A FACT

Today, the American Red Cross collects more than 6 million units of blood each year. Each unit contains 15 ounces (445 milliliters) of blood and 2 ounces (60 milliliters) of solution to help preserve it. When someone donates blood, it is carefully screened for diseases before it is stored by blood type.

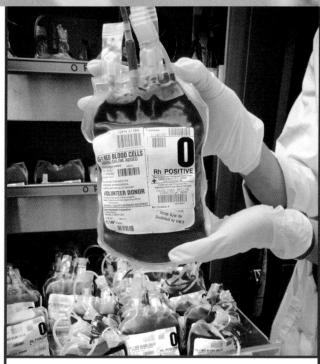

The various parts of blood are prepared and packaged for use at a blood bank.

After the War

Years later, Drew returned to work at Howard University, where he had begun his medical career as a resident. This time he returned as the chief of staff and medical director. By 1950, Drew had trained more than half of the African American surgeons in the United States.

On April 1, 1950, Drew was in a serious automobile accident in North Carolina. At that time, hospitals in the South were still segregated. The closest hospital to the site of Drew's accident was for white people only.

However, doctors there helped Drew. He was given a transfusion with blood from a blood bank. Sadly, Drew could not be saved. He died at the hospital. He was only 45 years old.

Although blood banks could not save Drew's life, his invention saved the lives of countless other people. Today, several societies honor the work of Charles Drew. One society at Amherst College helps students who are interested in careers in medicine. In Los Angeles, California, The Charles R. Drew University of Medicine and Science prepares students for careers in medicine.

A stamp honoring Charles Drew was released in 2001 as part of a series of stamps honoring American doctors.

Charles R Drew MD

USA 35c

Charles R. Drew University of Medicine and Science

CAREERS IN MEDICINE

Will you become one of tomorrow's medical pioneers? Here are some careers you might pursue.

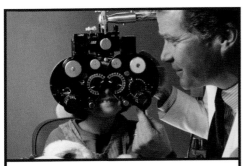

EYE DOCTOR
- Examines patients' eyes to determine if they need glasses
- Knows about diseases of the eye and methods of treating them

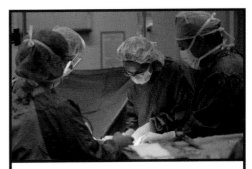

SURGEON
- Specializes in operating on organs
- Knows the structure and function of the body
- Examines and fixes organs

PHYSICAL THERAPIST
- Helps people recover from injury or disease
- Works closely with patients to help them regain movement after an accident or strengthen their muscles after surgery

NURSE
- Enjoys helping people get well
- Works in a hospital or clinic
- Teaches people how to stay healthy and protect themselves from disease

GLOSSARY

antibiotic	(an-tee-by-AH-tik) a substance that kills or harms bacteria
antiseptic	(an-tih-SEP-tik) a substance that is used to clean wounds and kill bacteria
bacteria	(bak-TEER-ee-uh) tiny organisms, some of which cause disease
bacteriologist	(bak-teer-ee-AH-luh-jist) someone who studies bacteria
blood bank	(BLUD BANK) a place where blood or plasma is stored for future use
blood transfusion	(BLUD trans-FYOO-zhun) the introduction of blood into the body
field hospital	(FEELD HAHS-pih-tul) a temporary hospital set up near a battlefield
inoculation	(ih-NAH-kyuh-LAY-shun) an injection that contains a vaccine
lysozyme	(LY-suh-zime) a natural substance found in tears and saliva
penicillin	(peh-nih-SIH-lin) a natural substance made by the mold *Penicillium notatum*, which acts as an antibiotic
plasma	(PLAZ-muh) the liquid part of the blood
segregated	(SEH-grih-gate-ed) separated from a group
spore	(SPOR) a tiny structure produced by molds and other living things
vaccine	(vak-SEEN) a substance containing dead or weakened forms of bacteria or viruses given to a person to help build up resistance to the disease

INDEX